HEATHERS
AND HEATHS

ALAN TOOGOOD

HarperCollins*Publishers*

Products mentioned in this book

Benlate* + 'Activex'	contains	benomyl
'Keriroot'	contains	NAA + captan
'Weedol'	contains	diquat-paraquat

Products marked thus 'Sybol' are trade marks of Imperial Chemical Industries plc
'Benlate' is a registered trade mark of Du Pont's
Read the label before you buy; use pesticides safely

Editors Maggie Daykin, Susanne Mitchell
Designer Chris Walker
Production Controller Craig Chubb
Picture research Moira McIlroy

First published 1989 by
HarperCollins Publishers

This edition published 1992

© Marshall Cavendish Limited 1989, 1992

A CIP catalogue record for this book is available from the British Library.

Photoset by Litho Link Ltd., Welshpool, Powys, Wales
Printed and bound in Hong Kong by Dai Nippon Printing Company

Front cover: Heather garden in summer by Michael Warren
Back cover: Calluna vulgaris 'Wickwar Flame' by The Harry Smith
Horticultural Photographic Collection

CONTENTS

INTRODUCTION

The heaths and heathers, evergreen shrubs related to rhododendrons and azaleas (they are in the *Ericaceae* family), are one of the few groups of plants capable of providing colour and interest all the year round. A collection of the different kinds will provide flowers and foliage colour throughout all four seasons.

Although we use the terms heath and heather very loosely, 'heath' really refers to *Erica* and *Daboecia*, two of the genera.

The ericas are mainly low mat-forming plants, although some – the so-called tree heaths – grow into quite tall shrubs (not trees as such). Ericas have short needle-like foliage and spikes of small but pleasing bell-shaped flowers.

Daboecias have larger bell-shaped flowers and their foliage is elliptic – rather like that of privet, although on a much smaller scale – and deep shiny green.

The third genus, *Calluna*, is popularly known as 'heather'. As with most ericas and daboecias, the habit is mat-forming. The foliage, however, is very different; small and scale-like, the individual leaves being packed very closely together. The flowers are again bell-shaped and carried in spikes.

These, then, are the heaths and heathers – there are no other genera. Between them they can provide flowers all the year round, even in the depth of winter, and varieties with coloured foliage – such as gold – look good all year round but they show up especially well in winter.

Adaptable Heaths and heathers look at home in gardens of any style, from modern formal town gardens to informal country gardens. They also associate well with modern architecture and paving. In informal country gardens, plantings of heaths and heathers may well echo the surrounding countryside – perhaps heathland or moorland where heaths and heathers grow wild.

A very good incentive for growing heaths and heathers has already been given – the all-year-round colour they provide. But there are several other reasons why this group of plants can be recommended.

Heaths and heathers are suitable for all sizes of garden. Even the

To confound a fairly common belief that heaths and heathers can all look pretty well alike, here's proof that they are not! *Erica vagans* 'Valerie Proudley' teamed with *Calluna vulgaris* 'Darkness' and *Erica cinerea* 'Pink Ice' provide contrast in colour and form yet work together brilliantly.

6

tiniest plot can accommodate at least a few different kinds. If you garden only on a balcony you can grow them in containers.

They can be grown in all kinds of soil, too. It is true that the majority must have acid or lime-free soil, but some will grow in alkaline (limy or chalky) conditions, particularly the winter-flowering ericas. If your soil is not right for some of them, then why not grow a collection in pots, tubs or window-boxes?

Labour-saving One of the great advantages of heaths and heathers is that they are labour-saving, needing minimum attention once planted. This is a boon to owners of medium to large gardens, for a generous bed of heaths and heathers ensures that a good part of the garden can be left to its own devices yet still be highly attractive.

Once planted, heaths and heathers will retain their appeal for many years, but eventually they start to become straggly and this is the time to replant them, perhaps with young plants you have raised from cuttings – propagation is really quite easy (see page 12).

A thick carpet of multi-coloured ericas, here offset by a background of conifers, is an attractive solution to keeping down weeds in a large open space. Planned with care, it can also provide year-round colour.

SOILS AND PLANTING

Provide the right conditions for heaths and heathers and you will find them very easy to grow. Choose an open part of the garden with full sun and make sure there are no tree branches overhanging the site. Most kinds tolerate exposed windy conditions – indeed this is characteristic of the natural habitats of many heaths and heathers.

Whatever your soil type, there's a heath or heather, or both, that can be planted there. Just consider some of their natural habitats. What they will not tolerate is wet, waterlogged conditions. See how well this mixed planting of *Erica cinerea* is responding to a well-drained, sunny location.

Before planting heaths and heathers carry out a soil test with one of the inexpensive soil-testing kits, to determine whether your soil is acid (free from lime or chalk) or alkaline (limy or chalky).

Soil types Acid soil will enable you to grow the complete range of heaths and heathers. If it is alkaline, however, your choice will be limited to a few of the ericas, mainly winter-flowering kinds.

Acidity/alkalinity is measured on the pH scale. Soil with a pH of 7 is neutral and suitable for lime-tolerant heathers; below pH7 is acid while above is alkaline.

The soil needs to be well-drained, as heaths and heathers will not tolerate very wet or waterlogged conditions. However, some grow naturally in sites with permanently moist soils.

Clay soils are perfectly suitable provided the drainage is good. Sandy soils are ideal as they are very well-drained – indeed sandy soils are natural habitats of many heaths and heathers.

The lime-tolerant kinds can be grown in shallow chalky soils; at least the drainage is good. Peaty soils are also suitable and, again, often form the natural habitats of some heaths and heathers.

Peaty soils can be very moist so choose suitable kinds to plant – see the descriptive lists starting on page 28 for guidance on this.

Improving Soils First eradicate all perennial weeds by spraying them when in full growth with a weed-killer containing glyphosate. When they are dead, dig the soil thoroughly to at least the depth of the spade. Dig to two depths if you need to improve drainage, also adding plenty of grit.

All soils (with the exception of the naturally peaty kinds) will benefit from the addition of peat, leafmould or pulverized bark such as 'Forest Bark' Ground and Composted Bark; these are especially important for light, very well-drained soils.

Before planting, apply a base dressing of blood, fish and bone fertilizer.

Buying and planting Heathers are bought in containers from garden centres or specialist growers. One-year-old plants are the most economical; two-year-olds are about twice the price.

The ideal planting times are April and May, or September and October, when the soil is moist and warm so the plants rapidly establish. You can plant between June and August but bear in mind that the soil can dry out rapidly so be prepared to water regularly.

Before planting, ensure the rootballs of the plants are thoroughly moist. If you plant dry rootballs the plants may fail to establish.

Carefully remove the container and set the plant in a hole slightly larger than the rootball. Replace the soil around it and firm moderately with your fingers.

It is important to plant the optimum per m^2 (square yard) as indicated in the descriptive lists, if you want the plants to form a dense mat within a couple of years.

ABOVE If in doubt about what type of soil you have, consider buying one of the easy-to-use soil-testing kits. A solution of a small sample of your soil dropped into a chemical colours according to its type. The garden may have varying soil, so test in more than one place.

RIGHT Correct spacing is crucial to dense cover.

AFTERCARE

Although heaths and heathers are generally regarded as being labour-saving plants, a little regular attention as outlined below will ensure that you get the best from them.

Mulching is highly recommended as it slows down evaporation of moisture from the soil and suppresses the growth of annual weeds. A mulch is a 2.5-5cm (1-2in) layer of organic matter spread over the surface of the soil.

The best material to use for mulching heaths and heathers is sphagnum peat; 'Forest Bark' Ground and Composted Bark is suitable, too. Both materials should be moistened before use, and the soil must be moist and weed-free when you lay the mulch.

Mulch immediately after planting and top it up annually, if necessary, in the spring. It should be said that bark lasts longer than peat.

Watering Never allow the soil to dry out, particularly with newly planted heaths and heathers. Apply water gently, with a sprinkler, as soon as the top 2.5cm (1in) of soil starts to become dry.

Apply enough water to penetrate the soil to a depth of 15cm (6in). This means about 27 litres of water per m² (4¾ galls per sq yd), which is the equivalent of 2.5cm (1in) of rain. Place some empty tins on the site before you begin watering – when there is 2.5cm of water in the bottom of these you will know that you have applied enough.

Feeding Heaths and heathers do not need a great deal of feeding. In April each year an application of blood, fish and bone fertilizer, at 56-85g per m² (2-3oz per sq yd), will keep them happy. It should be lightly hoed into the soil or mulch.

One of the many delights of heathers and heaths is that you don't have to dead-head by hand. Just lightly lop off the dead flowers with a pair of shears.

10

New plantings will quickly form a thick mat that in itself is a good suppressor of weeds, but a layer of mulch will also slow down evaporation of moisture from the soil without impairing essential drainage.

Weeding Very little will be needed if you keep the plants mulched. If the odd weed does appear in the mulch, simply pull it out by hand.

With un-mulched plants, either hand weed or hoe very shallowly when the weeds are in the seedling stage. Alternatively, you could treat with 'Weedol'. Deep hoeing would damage the roots of plants you are trying to conserve.

Planted at optimum distances, heaths and heathers will eventually close up, forming a dense carpet that will successfully suppress all further weed growth.

Dense growth of weeds will retard the growth of heaths and heathers so do not allow this to occur.

Trimming The dead flower heads should be removed but never cut into old wood as this can kill the plants. Lightly trim off dead blooms with garden shears. Summer- and autumn-flowering plants can be trimmed in spring (the dead blooms look attractive over winter). Winter- and spring-flowering plants should both be trimmed immediately after they have flowered.

Pests and diseases Heaths and heathers are troubled by very few pests and diseases. Rabbits can nibble shoots, in which case the bed will have to be surrounded by wire netting (or better still use wire all round the garden), burying it 15cm (6in) below the surface. Alternatively, you could use a proprietary animal repellant – but you will have to keep re-applying this.

Ericas and callunas are prone to heather die-back, a soil-borne fungal disease which attacks the roots and base of plants. Grey areas are noticeable on foliage, and shoots often die back. Ideally, one should dig up and burn affected plants and replace the

Shoots still attached to the parent plant can be encouraged to form healthy roots by the process of layering. Use either 'mound' layering, as described in the text, or the method shown right, in which lower shoots are carefully bent and buried.

soil with a fresh supply before replanting. Alternatively, spray with Benlate + 'Activex' and repeat two or three weeks later. Combine this with foliar feeding during the summer.

Propagation Heaths and heathers will need replacing with young plants when they become old, woody and cease to flower well. Fortunately, they are easily increased from cuttings or by layering so you could have batches of young plants ready to replace older ones.

Cuttings are prepared from semi-ripe shoots in the summer; use young side shoots that are ripening or becoming woody at the base but are still soft at the tips.

Propagation can be spread out over the summer. For instance, in early summer take cuttings of *Erica arborea, E. erigena (E. mediterranea), E. herbacea (E. carnea), E. × darleyensis* and *E. vagans.*

In mid to late summer take cuttings of *Erica ciliaris, E. cinerea, E. tetralix* and summer-flowering hybrids.

During later summer and early autumn you can propagate *Calluna*

vulgaris and *Daboecia cantabrica.*

When shoots are 3-5cm (1½-2in) long, carefully pull them off with a piece of the old wood attached (this is called a heel). With the exception of callunas, which have minute scale-like leaves, carefully strip off all the leaves from the lower half of the cuttings, using finger and thumb. The tips of the cuttings can be pinched out, although this is not essential. Dip the base of each cutting in Benlate solution to protect it from fungal rot, then dip it in a hormone rooting powder such as 'Keriroot'.

Cuttings are inserted in seed trays containing cutting compost: equal parts of moist peat and sharp sand (parts by volume). You should get 100 cuttings in a standard-size seed tray. Insert them up to the lower leaves in holes made with a dibber or pencil. Lightly firm them and then water in.

Cuttings can be rooted in a propagating case or mist-propagation unit, with a basal temperature of 21°C (70°F). Rooting will start within two weeks, when the cuttings should be removed to the greenhouse bench. Cuttings will root in a garden frame, but they will naturally take longer to do so.

Pot off rooted cuttings into 7.5cm (3in) pots, using acid or ericaceous compost. Overwinter in a well-ventilated garden frame and plant in the garden when one year old.

Layering encourages shoots to form roots while still attached to the parent plant. This is done in mid-spring and shoots will be rooted by the autumn.

Lift the parent plant carefully, retaining a good ball of soil around the roots. Replant in a deeper hole so that the lower half of the stems is below ground level. Spread out the stems while replanting, working fine soil between them. Keep the plant moist throughout summer.

In autumn, lift and cut off all of the rooted shoots, pot off and then treat as for rooted cuttings.

If the parent plant is trimmed back and replanted it stands a good chance of surviving.

RIGHT AND BELOW Prepare cuttings in summer, using young side shoots. Dip the base in a rooting compound then plant round pot's perimeter and cover with polythene.

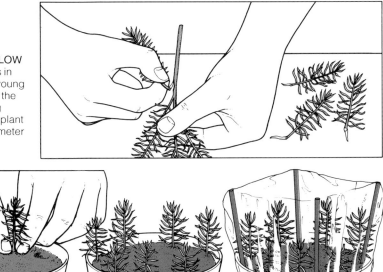

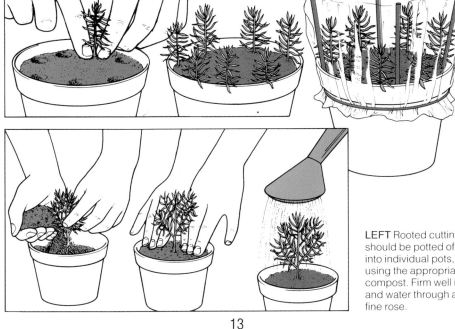

LEFT Rooted cuttings should be potted off into individual pots, using the appropriate compost. Firm well in and water through a fine rose.

COLOUR ALL THE YEAR

The most usual way of growing heaths and heathers is in a bed on their own. Ideally, it should be of an informal, irregular shape with gently flowing and curving edges. A heather bed makes a superb feature in a lawn but can also be included in a paved area.

Even a small lawn can take a colourful island of low-growing heathers and heaths, here interplanted with begonias and a conifer. Mowing should present no problems if you select compact forms.

If space permits, each variety should be planted in a bold irregular shaped group, up to 1m² (1 sq yd) in area, so creating a patchwork effect in the bed. Choose a sufficiently wide range of different kinds to ensure colour and interest are provided throughout the year.

A bed on acid soil should certainly feature in the summer some groups of *Calluna vulgaris* (ling) varieties. Many of these are extremely free-flowering; try, for example, the pink 'County Wicklow', 'Elsie Purnell' or 'J. H. Hamilton'.

Another important heather for summer is *Erica cinerea* (bell heather), with a carpeting habit of growth, and very free-flowering in varieties such as pink 'Cevennes', 'Purple Beauty', and 'Pink Ice'.

Varieties of *Erica vagans* (Cornish heath) should be included for summer. Among bushy plants with a very floriferous habit are the very popular 'Lyonesse', white; 'Mrs D. F. Maxwell', pink; and 'St Keverne', rose-pink.

Erica tetralix (cross-leaved heath) varieties are rather unusual and have greyish or silvery foliage. The leaves cross over each other, hence the common name. Recommended varieties for a summer display include crimson 'Con Underwood' and 'Pink Star'.

Contrasting well with these heaths and heathers in texture and shape are the varieties of *Daboecia cantabrica* (St Dabeoc's heath), distinguished by their larger leaves and flowers. Some good varieties are 'Praegerae', which is a dark pink,

14

and 'William Buchanan', crimson.

With a good selection of summer-flowering heaths and heathers we do not have to worry too much about autumn colour, for many of these varieties continue flowering into early or mid-autumn. However, *Calluna vulgaris* varieties particularly noted for their autumn flower display include 'H. E. Beale' and 'Peter Sparkes', both with double pink flowers.

The coloured-foliage varieties of *Calluna vulgaris* really come into their own in winter, the mainly golden leaves shining in the pale winter sunshine. Among the best are 'Beoley Gold'; 'Blazeaway' in red and orange; 'Gold Haze'; 'Joy Vanstone'; 'Orange Queen'; multi-coloured 'Robert Chapman'; silver-grey 'Silver Queen'; and 'Sir John Charrington'.

Varieties of *Erica* × *darleyensis* and *E. herbacea* (*E. carnea*) are essential for their winter flowers and you will find that they continue into spring. Some good varieties are recommended under A Bed for Alkaline Soil (see page 16).

A choice grouping of *Chamaecyparis* 'Boulevard' with *Erica cinerea* 'Pink Ice' and the spiky golden foliage of *Calluna vulgaris* 'Gold Flame', which looks particularly striking in pale, winter sunlight.

Massed rose-purple flowers of *Erica australis*, a large shrub that lends height to a bed of mixed heathers and heaths. In Portugal, this shrub grows wild and flower colour varies; some have been collected with a view to cultivating them and thus extending the colour choice.

The dead flowers of many of the summer-flowering heaths and heathers make an attractive feature over winter, as they are in russet or buff shades, so do not trim them off until the spring.

Some plants for spring flowers, and also to give variation in height in the heather bed, include *Erica arborea* 'Alpina' (tree heath), which forms a large shrub bearing fragrant white flowers. Two other large shrubs are *E. australis* (Spanish heath) with rose-purple blooms, and *E. lusitanica* (Portugal or tree heath) with fragrant white flowers.

The spring-flowering *Erica erigena (E. mediterranea)* varieties are much lower, bushy plants. The purple-red 'Brightness' is a well-known and justly popular variety.

A bed for alkaline soil We are much more restricted here in choice of types but it is still possible to have colour and interest all the year round in limy or chalky conditions. However, the main display will be in the winter and spring, from varieties of *Erica × darleyensis* and *E. herbacea (E. carnea)*. Both form carpets of growth and flower very freely over a long period. Those which are at their best in winter include *E. × darleyensis* varieties 'Darley Dale', pink, and 'Silberschmelse' ('Molten Silver'), white; and *E. herbacea* varieties 'King George', pink; 'Springwood Pink', 'Springwood White' and 'Vivellii', bright carmine.

Erica × darleyensis varieties which bloom in spring include red-purple 'Jack H. Brummage'. Spring-flowering *E. herbacea* varieties include 'Myretoun Ruby' and 'Ruby Glow', both with ruby-red flowers.

Varieties of spring-flowering *Erica erigena (E. mediterranea)* (Mediterranean heath) will grow in alkaline soils. A good variety is 'W. T. Rackliff', which has fresh white flowers.

Tolerating *slightly* alkaline soils is the spring-blooming *Erica australis* (Spanish heath). It gives variation in height in the bed and has rose-purple flowers.

Also tolerating *slightly* alkaline soils is *Erica lusitanica* (Portugal or tree heath) with white blooms in spring, again ideal for providing variation in height. A little-known heath that thrives in alkaline soils and produces pink flowers in spring

is *Erica umbellata* (Portuguese heath). Unfortunately, it is not very hardy and can be recommended only for areas with mild winters.

Summer flower colour can be provided by *Erica terminalis (E. stricta, E. corsica)* (Corsican heath) which grows well in alkaline conditions. This medium-size shrub is ideal for providing variation in height, and bears pink flowers that continue into early autumn.

Do not forget that the coloured foliage varieties of *Erica herbacea (E. carnea)* will provide colour all the year round and will be conspicuous in summer and autumn when there are few plants in flower. Highly recommended are 'Ann Sparkes', 'Foxhollow', 'January Sun' and 'Westwood Yellow', all of which have golden foliage.

The aptly named *Erica carnea* 'Myretoun Ruby' gives a brilliant display from January to mid-May. The dark green foliage is completely hidden by massed flowers to a height of 20cm (8in).

PLANT ASSOCIATIONS

Heaths and heathers do not associate well with many other plants, so, if you want mixed planting schemes featuring heathers, choose plants which are found growing naturally with them in the wild, such as birches, gorse, brooms and pines. Most of the companion plants described here will grow in acid or alkaline soils, but some heathers will only succeed in acid conditions, so bear this in mind when planning groups. Refer to the descriptive lists for soil conditions.

The popular idea of growing heaths and heathers on their own, in informal heather beds, has been described in the previous chapter. However, many gardeners include dwarf specimen conifers in these beds for contrast in shape, texture and colour and to provide variation in height (most heaths and heathers are by habit low mat-forming or carpeting plants).

Recommended plants There is a vast range of dwarf conifers that make attractive companions for heathers. Here is a small selection of the very best.

Abies procera 'Glauca Prostrata' (dwarf noble fir) is one of the 'blue' conifers, with grey-blue foliage, which contrast so well in colour with heaths and heathers (especially golden-foliage varieties). It has a low prostrate habit and definitely needs acid soil.

Very popular is *Chamaecyparis lawsoniana* 'Ellwoodii' (Lawson cypress), a cone-shaped plant with grey-green foliage (yellow-flushed in *C.l.* 'Ellwood's Gold').

Forming a wide cone of brilliant silver-blue foliage – a marvellous contrast to heathers – is *Chamaecyparis pisifera* 'Boulevard' (sawara cypress). Not at its best when grown in alkaline soils, however.

Chamaecyparis pisifera 'Filifera Aurea' will eventually make a medium to large shrub, but it is fairly slow growing and its attractive golden foliage makes it an ideal companion for heaths and heathers.

Pinus mugo 'Mops' is a particularly reliable dwarf form of the mountain pine. Its grey-green foliage and winter buds provide a good contrast to winter-flowering heathers and heaths.

Chamaecyparis pisifera 'Filifera Aurea' (sawara cypress) associates well with grey-leaved heaths and forms a dome of filamentous yellow foliage. Again, this is not at its best in alkaline soils.

Forming a wide cone of grey-green or blue-green prickly foliage, is *Juniperus chinensis* 'Pyramidalis' (Chinese juniper).

Several dwarf piceas are recommended for heather beds, including *Picea glauca* 'Albertiana Conica' (white spruce), which forms a neat cone of vivid green foliage. *Picea pungens* 'Globosa' (dwarf Colorado spruce) shows up from afar with its light silver-blue foliage. It is a very bushy, dome-shaped plant.

Dwarf pines are recommended for planting in heather beds. They include, for example, *Pinus leucodermis* 'Compact Gem' (dwarf Bosnian pine), a dome-shaped plant with dark green needles (leaves). *P. mugo* 'Gnom' and 'Mops' (dwarf mountain pines) are dome-shaped, with green needles. *P. strobus* 'Nana' (dwarf Weymouth pine) has a spreading habit and attractive bluish-green needles.

Forming a dome of soft feathery foliage is *Thuja orientalis* 'Rosedalis' (Chinese arbor-vitae). The foliage is yellow in spring and purple-brown in winter.

One of the most popular dwarf golden conifers is *Thuja occidentalis* 'Rheingold' (dwarf white cedar), which forms a wide dome of foliage.

Mixed borders Borders containing shrubs, perennials, bulbs and other plants are very popular in today's gardens. There are many ways of designing them, including having groups of plants which provide colour and interest during particular seasons. Heaths and heathers can also be included in some of these groupings.

A group for winter There is certainly no lack of plants for winter colour and, of course, the winter-flowering heaths can feature in such a plan.

The main 'framework' of the group could consist of *Prunus subhirtella* 'Autumnalis' (autumn cherry), a small tree with semi-double white flowers. This will need a dark background to show off the flowers, such as the evergreen shrub *Viburnum tinus* (laurustinus) with white blooms in winter/spring. A witch hazel could also be included, such as *Hamamelis mollis* 'Pallida' with pale yellow spidery flowers.

At the front of this group, arrange drifts or bold groups of winter-flowering heathers: varieties of *Erica herbacea (E. carnea)* and *E. × darleyensis*. And, if the soil is acid, include *Calluna vulgaris* (ling) varieties with coloured foliage like 'Blazeaway', red and orange; 'Beoley Gold', brilliant gold, and 'Robert Chapman', red and yellow.

ABOVE Heathers need not be restricted to their own bed. Here, a planting of heathers lends its rich mixture of colours to the front of a long border.

LEFT Even in the depth of winter, this large garden in Kent is as colourful as in spring or summer, thanks to a planting of mixed heaths.

Spring and summer group Birches associate well with heaths and heathers, so one of these could help to form the framework of a spring and summer group. Birches with very white stems include *Betula jacquemontii, B.* 'Jermyns' and *B. platyphylla szechuanica*, all medium-sized trees. Or why not try the new *Betula* 'Golden Cloud', with golden foliage and white bark.

Shrubs recommended for this group include the double-flowered gorse, *Ulex europaeus* 'Plenus', a small shrub with yellow flowers for acid soils; *Genista aetnensis* (Mount Etna broom) is a large shrub with yellow flowers; and *Cytisus scoparius* (common broom) varieties are medium shrubs best grown in acid soils. Dwarf pines, such as *Pinus strobus* 'Nana' or *P. leucodermis* 'Compact Gem', could be planted at the front of this group and drifting through these summer-flowering heathers such as varieties of *Calluna vulgaris, Erica cinerea* and *Erica vagans*.

Autumn group A group for autumn could include a shrub noted for autumn colour, such as *Euonymus europaeus* 'Red Cascade'. This medium-sized shrub has bunches of pink-red seed capsules which open to reveal bright orange seeds. The foliage also takes on brilliant tints. Around this shrub have drifts of autumn-flowering heathers: *Calluna vulgaris* varieties such as 'H. E. Beale' and 'Peter Sparkes'. Between these groups of heathers plant clumps of autumn-flowering crocuses: *Crocus kotschyanus*, mauve-blue flowers; *C. laevigatus*, pale blue, and *C. speciosus*, mauve-blue, or forms in various shades of blue as well as white.

If you have the space for the large leaves to develop in the spring, you could also include colchicums (popularly called autumn crocus), with crocus-like flowers in autumn. Good species include *Colchicum autumnale*, which has mauve-blue flowers, and *C. speciosum*, mauve or white.

ABOVE Bright summer heathers, here offset by a well-kept lawn – the perfect foil for such boldness.

LEFT In a spring garden, heathers vie for attention with golden daffodils.

On the rock garden The rock garden is usually devoid of colour in the winter but not so if you include some varieties of *Erica herbacea (E. carnea),* the winter-flowering heather. It looks well with delicate alpines and indeed is itself a mountain dweller, found in pastures and on the edge of pine woodland on mountainsides. Plant groups between rocks and combine them with miniature winter-flowering cyclamen.

These cyclamen are diminutive versions of the popular florists' cyclamen but, unlike that, are perfectly hardy. Try *Cyclamen × atkinsii* with its silver-marbled foliage and red, pink or white flowers; and *C. coum,* also with silver-marbled leaves and pink, red or white flowers.

These miniature cyclamen, which associate so well with winter-flowering heathers, would appreciate the shade cast by rocks whereas the heathers need full sun.

Winter-flowering crocuses could actually be planted among the heathers so that they grow up through them. Suitable kinds include the *Crocus chrysanthus* varieties which come in various colours such as shades of yellow, blue and white; *C. imperati* with its purple flowers; and *C. tomasinianus,* mauve flowers.

Ground-cover schemes The low-growing carpeting or mat-forming heaths and heathers make ideal ground cover in various parts of the garden provided the site is open and sunny. They do not have to be grown alone, though.

A scheme which can be highly recommended is to grow *Clematis viticella* hybrids over winter-flowering heathers, to provide further colour when the heathers have finished flowering. These small-flowered clematis bloom from mid-summer until early autumn and should be allowed to trail over the carpet of heathers. As they produce only a light canopy of foliage they will enhance rather than harm the heathers.

Even in deepest winter, the rock garden need not be devoid of colour. When delicate alpine plants are taking their rest, a planting of winter-flowering heathers can admirably fill the void. Take care that they are not too overshadowed by larger rocks.

Many *Clematis viticella* hybrids can be used over heathers, including 'Abundance', with dark pink flowers and 'Alba Luxurians', white. 'Etoile Violette' with dark violet flowers and 'Royal Velours', which has very dark purple blooms, look lovely growing over golden-leaved heathers. 'Rubra', dark red, and 'Venosa Violacea', purple and white, are two other very compatible plants.

The *Clematis viticella* hybrids can also be grown over summer-flowering heathers if desired, again choosing varieties which contrast or harmonize in colour.

Within the planting of heathers the clematis should be spaced 1.5m (5ft) apart each way. However, do allow the heathers to establish well before planting the clematis – give them a year or 18 months to settle down and grow. Leave gaps among the heathers in which to plant the clematis later.

Prune the clematis in late autumn by cutting back the stems really hard. This will give the winter-flowering heather the chance to bloom properly rather than be smothered in dead, soggy foliage.

ABOVE A perfect partnership. The crisp white *Crocus chrysanthus* 'Snow Bunting' set among the even more diminutive flowers of a carpeting heather.

RIGHT The small, star-shaped flowers of *Clematis viticella* 'Venosa Violacea' can be grown over the summer-flowering heathers, provided that you allow the latter to establish themselves before planting the clematis.

CONTAINER GROWING

One of the most popular aspects of gardening today is growing plants in ornamental containers. Never before has such a wide range of containers been available, and there are few gardens without a tub, window-box or hanging basket. Heaths and heathers, perhaps in association with dwarf conifers, can be grown in tubs, large pots and window-boxes and make for labour-saving displays and a pleasant change from very time-consuming seasonal bedding.

Calluna vulgaris 'Kinlochruel' is a neat, compact form suitable for containers and its tiny white flowers would fit in with any colour scheme.

For heathers, it matters little whether containers are in wood, terracotta or reconstituted stone. Simply choose a material and style that is appropriate to both the house and the garden.

However, glazed containers and those made from plastic are not recommended, for they are non-porous and the compost is inclined to remain too moist for heathers.

Adequate depth is important, to ensure that the compost does not dry out rapidly. For tubs and pots the depth should be at least 30cm (1ft) and preferably 45cm (18in). Window-boxes should have a minimum depth measurement of 25cm (10in).

Large tubs When it comes to planting schemes, one is rather restricted by the size of the container. However, a pleasing scheme consists of a dwarf cone- or dome-shaped conifer in the centre, surrounded by small compact heathers. Or, if the container is against a wall and is viewed only from the 'front', then have a conifer – or group of conifers – at the back with heathers in front.

Suitable small or compact heathers for containers include varieties of *Calluna vulgaris* such as 'Golden Carpet', 'Kinlochruel', 'Multicolor' and 'Tib'. Varieties of *Erica herbacea (E. carnea)* include 'January Sun', 'Springwood Pink' and 'Springwood

White'. All of these are described in the next chapter.

Suitable dwarf conifers include *Chamaecyparis lawsoniana* 'Ell-woodii', a greyish-green cone; and

C.l. 'Ellwood's Pillar', a narrow blue-grey cone. *Juniperus communis* 'Compressa', a narrow grey-green cone, may be too small, unless you buy a fairly old specimen. *Picea glauca* 'Albertiana Conica', bright green wide cone; and *Taxus baccata* 'Fastigiata Aurea' (golden Irish yew), narrow yellow-green column, will become too tall for the tub eventually.

Troughs and window-boxes Long containers such as troughs and window-boxes can also be planted with a combination of heathers and dwarf conifers recommended above.

There are one or two arrange-ments that could be used. For instance, a cone-shaped conifer, or a group, could be planted at one end, following on with heathers. If space permits, you could have a spreading conifer at the other end, such as a

ABOVE *Calluna vulgaris* 'Multicolor' is another ideal plant for containers, whether as the focal point or as framework planting. Position it close to the edge, where it can 'trail' slightly.

RIGHT Take care to secure your window-box before you plant it up and if necessary mount it on blocks for ease of drainage.

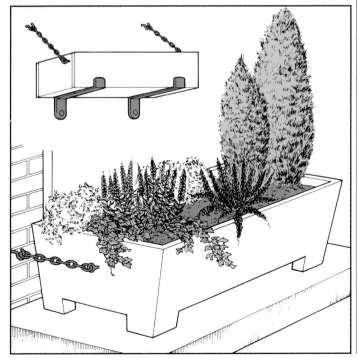

25

Juniperus horizontalis variety (say, the grey-blue 'Bar Harbor'); or *Juniperus squamata* 'Blue Carpet' with silver-blue foliage. Both of these junipers will eventually become too large for containers but they can then be planted in the garden if you wish.

Another idea is to have a cone-shaped conifer – or a group – in the centre of the trough or window-box, with heathers on either side. Bear in mind, though, that this arrangement in a window-box may reduce light indoors.

For spring colour, miniature bulbs could be grown through the heathers. Several kinds are suitable, such as the starry blue scillas and chionodoxas. Snowdrops are admirable and, of course, produce their welcome white bells in the winter. Small crocuses can be recommended, too, such as the many varieties of *Crocus chrysanthus*. None of these little bulbs produces excessive foliage so the heathers will not be swamped by them. Remember to leave the foliage until it dies down; then it can be cut off. This will ensure that the bulbs get sufficient nourishment to flower well in the following year.

Miniature bulbs can, of course, also be used in tubs and large pots.

Planting containers First of all make sure the containers have drainage holes in the bottom. Most do, but occasionally one comes across a container without. This would result in waterlogged compost which spells death to heathers (and indeed to all container plants).

Before adding compost, position the container where you want it – a filled container is obviously more difficult to move. Remember to position it in an open sunny spot where plants can thrive.

Next place a layer of drainage material in the bottom of the container, to about 2.5cm (1in) in depth. The best material for this purpose is broken clay flower pots (known as crocks). Place some large pieces over the drainage holes, then add a layer of smaller pieces. To prevent compost from washing down into the drainage layer and blocking it, cover the crocks with a thin layer of rough leafmould or peat.

Use a peat-based or soilless compost for heathers and conifers. Remember it should be acid. A proprietary ericaceous compost (formulated for lime-hating plants) would be ideal.

Partially fill the container with compost and firm it very lightly. Remove the plants from their pots and arrange them on the compost, ensuring that the top of the rootballs (which should be moist) are at least 2.5cm (1in) below the rim of the

FAR LEFT When planting up containers always check that there are sufficient drainage holes. Place a generous layer of crocks in the base and cover these with peat or leafmould, then an ericaceaous compost to about 2.5cm (1in) below the rim.

LEFT Plant your chosen plants in the compost, carefully holding each one upright while adding more compost round its base. Firm well in, level surface and water.

container. Then fill in around the rootballs with more compost, again firming lightly. Ensure that the surface of the compost is at least 2.5cm (1in) below the rim of the container to allow room for watering. The tops of the rootballs should be only lightly covered with the compost.

When planting is complete give a thorough watering through a fine rose in order to settle the compost around the plants.

Aftercare On no account allow the compost to dry out completely or plants will certainly suffer and may even drop their foliage. If this happens, plants will not recover. As soon as the top 2.5cm (1in) of compost is dry give a thorough watering. Apply sufficient so that it runs out of the bottom of the container; only then can you be sure that the entire volume of compost has been moistened. It is best to use rainwater if your tapwater is 'hard' (in other words, contains lime or chalk).

In the spring each year, topdress the compost with a sprinkling of organic fertilizer, such as blood, fish and bone.

Try not to allow the compost to freeze solid over long periods in the winter as this can result in the death of the plants. A good safeguard is to insulate the containers with straw or bracken, held in place with wire netting. Or transfer the containers to a frost-free (but cool) greenhouse for the winter.

When the heathers start to decline in vigour, and look old and untidy, replant with young plants. Completely empty the container and re-fill with fresh compost. At the same time, any conifers that are becoming too large can be planted in another part of the garden and replaced with smaller specimens.

HEATHERS IN SEASON

A carefully choosen collection of heaths and heathers will provide flowers all the year round. To help you make a choice, therefore, the varieties recommended have been grouped under flowering seasons, but bear in mind that flowering can overlap seasons. This selection also includes a good range with coloured foliage. As most heaths and heathers are planted in groups for bold effect the optimum number of plants per m^2 (square yard) has been given. These will quite quickly form a dense carpet.

SPRING

Erica arborea
(Tree heath) A tall erect bushy shrub up to 3.6m (12ft) high with a spread up to 2.4m (8ft). Brilliant green foliage and white, fragrant flowers. Only recommended for mild areas, and only in acid soil. Young plants should be staked.

'Alpina'
Similar to the species but has a stronger fragrance and is hardier.

Erica australis
(Spanish heath, southern tree heath) A tall erect shrub, reaching 1.8m (6ft) in height with a spread of 1.2m (4ft). Dark green foliage and fragrant rose-purple flowers. Grow in acid or *slightly* alkaline soil. Prone to wind and snow damage.

Fragrant *Erica arborea*

'Mr Robert'
White flowers and hardier than the species, otherwise similar.

Erica × darleyensis
(Winter-flowering heather) A hybrid, forming mats or carpets of foliage; excellent ground-cover. Flowers over a very long period. Only varieties are grown but there are many of them. Suitable for alkaline soils.

'Jack H. Brummage'
Red-purple flowers against a background of green foliage. Yellow-tipped shoots in spring. Rounded, bushy habit; height 45cm (18in).

Erica erigena (E. mediterranea)
(Mediterranean heath) Very bushy but usually with a compact, rounded habit. Generally, varieties are grown rather than the species. Excellent for alkaline soils but not excessively dry ones.

Erica erigena 'Brightness'

Erica herbacea 'Aurea' bears lilac-pink flowers

'Brightness'
Purple-red flowers and dark green foliage, tinted bronze in winter. Upright bushy habit, to 90cm (3ft) in height. Plant three per m^2 (sq yd).

'W. T. Rackliff'
White flowers set against vivid green foliage. Bushy, rounded habit; height 60cm (2ft). Plant three per m^2 (sq yd).

Erica herbacea (E. carnea)
(Winter-flowering heather) Mat-forming plant making excellent ground cover. Very long flowering period. Excellent for alkaline soils but if soil is very thin add a lot of peat. Only varieties are grown.

'Ann Sparkes'
Dark purple-red flowers and orange-yellow foliage; bronze-red shoot tips. Height 20cm (8in). Plant five of these per m^2 (sq yd).

'Aurea'
Deep pink blooms and golden-yellow foliage. Height 20cm (8in). Plant five per m^2 (sq yd).

'Foxhollow'
Flowers are lavender-coloured and rather sparse, but the foliage is brilliant gold in summer and tinged with red in winter. One of the best foliage varieties. Vigorous, spreading habit; height 15cm (6in). Plant three per m^2 (sq yd).

Erica herbacea 'Loughrigg'

'Loughrigg'
Dark pinkish-purple flowers. Dark green foliage, in winter flushed with bronze. Vigorous, erect habit, to a height of 20cm (8in). Plant five per m^2 (sq yd).

'Myretoun Ruby'
Glowing red flowers set against dark green foliage. Mat-forming, to a height of 20cm (8in). Plant five per m^2 (sq yd).

'Ruby Glow'
Glowing red flowers set against dark green foliage. Vigorous habit, to a height of 20cm (8in). Plant five per m^2 (sq yd).

'Westwood Yellow'
Lavender-coloured flowers, very freely produced, and beautiful golden-yellow foliage. Vigorous mat-forming habit; with a height of 15cm (6in). Plant five per m^2 (sq yd).

Erica lusitanica
(Portugal heath, tree heath) A large upright shrub to a height of 3m (10ft), with a spread of 90cm (3ft). Feathery, pale green foliage and fragrant white blooms, often starting to appear in winter. Best grown in acid soil but will succeed in *slightly* alkaline conditions. Severe frosts may kill back some of the growth but the plant generally makes a good recovery in spring.

Erica umbellata
(Portuguese heath) An upright, well-branched shrub to a height of 90cm (3ft) with a spread of 45cm (18in). Feathery, green foliage and dark pink blooms with deep brown anthers. This species is moderately hardy and recommended only for mild areas. Suitable for planting in alkaline soils.

Erica × *veitchii* 'Exeter'
(Tree heath) A large, vigorous shrub attaining a height of 2.4m (8ft) with a spread of 90cm (3ft). Feathery, vivid green foliage and plumes of fragrant white flowers, generally starting to appear in mid-winter. A tender species only recommended for outdoor cultivation in the mildest areas. Must be grown in acid soil.

Erica lusitanica (tree heath)

SUMMER

Calluna vulgaris
(Ling) A very well-known heather found growing wild in several parts of Britain. Distinguished by its very small scale-like leaves. Low carpet- or mat-forming habit, making excellent ground cover. Flowers carried in long spikes. The species is rarely grown, but there are hundreds of varieties, many with coloured foliage and flowers that are excellent for cutting. Acid soils only.

'Alba Plena'
Free-flowering, with double white blooms and mid-green foliage. Vigorous, dense habit of growth; height 50cm (20in). Plant five per m² (sq yd).

'Anne Marie'
Light pink flowers, deepening with age to dark rose-pink. Dark green foliage. Compact, bushy habit, to a height of 25cm (10in). Plant five of this variety per m² (sq yd).

Erica × veitchii 'Exeter'

Calluna vulgaris 'Beoley Gold'

'Beoley Gold'
White flowers but rather sparse; noted for its brilliant golden foliage, which is attractive throughout the year. Bushy habit, to a height of 30-40cm (12-15in). Plant five per m² (sq yd).

'Blazeaway'
The flowers are mauve; the foliage is deep red and orange in winter, but green during the summer. A rather loose, open plant, attaining a height of 50cm (20in). Plant five per m² (sq yd).

'Boskoop'
The flowers are lavender coloured and the foliage rich gold and orange, with attractive red tints in the winter. A low and compact grower – not more than 30cm (12in) in height. Plant five per m² (sq yd).

'County Wicklow'
One of the most popular varieties and highly recommended, this is an extremely free-flowering plant with double pink flowers and dark green foliage. A low, compact grower, no more than 25cm (10in) in height. Plant five per m² (sq yd).

'Elsie Purnell'
This is one of the top ten varieties of ling, with double flowers in rose-pink and beautiful grey-green foliage. Rather open in habit, attaining a height of 53cm (21in). Plant five per m² (sq yd).

'Gold Haze'
White flowers in long sprays, ideal for cutting for floral arrangements, and brilliant gold foliage that is attractive throughout the year. It also has a rather loose habit and attains a height of 50cm (20in). Plant five per m² (sq yd).

'Golden Carpet'
The flowers are reddish-purple, the foliage gold in summer and orange-red in winter. It is a slow grower with a prostrate habit, attaining a height of no more than 15cm (6in). Plant six per m² (sq yd).

'J. H. Hamilton'
This is undoubtedly one of the best varieties of ling for flowers, which are excellent for cutting for use in floral arrangements; it should be in every heather bed! The double flowers are bright pink and set against dark green leaves. It is vigorous in habit yet low-growing, forming a good carpet, no more than 25cm (10in) in height. Plant five per m² (sq yd).

'Joy Vanstone'
One of the best foliage varieties, this produces bright pink blooms but is grown primarily for its gold foliage, which becomes dark orange in the winter. Although on the tall side it is neat in habit; height 50cm (20in). Plant five per m² (sq yd).

'Kinlochruel'
The double flowers are white and set against dark green foliage; it is a plant especially recommended for containers due to its small size. A very low grower of compact, mounded habit, no more than 25cm (10in) in height. Plant five or six per m² (sq yd).

'Multicolor'
This is ideal for growing in ornamental containers. The flowers are purple but it is grown mainly for its foliage which changes colour with the seasons – yellow, orange, bronze and red. This small, compact plant is not more than 15cm (6in) in height. Plant seven per m² (sq yd).

Calluna vulgaris 'County Wicklow'

Calluna vulgaris 'Orange Queen', a highly popular heather

'Orange Queen'

Truly spectacular – should be in every heather bed! The blooms are lavender-coloured but this variety is grown mainly for its coloured foliage. It is deep yellow in spring, orange in summer and very deep orange in autumn and winter. Neat rounded habit to a height of 40cm (15in). Plant five per m^2 (sq yd).

'Robert Chapman'

This well-known variety produces purple flowers but is grown primarily for its colourful foliage, which changes with the seasons. It starts deep yellow, then turns to bronze, and eventually becomes yellow and red. An 'essential' variety. Dense habit of growth; height 40cm (16in). Plant six per m^2 (sq yd).

Calluna vulgaris 'Wickwar Flame'

'Silver Queen'
This variety produces purple blooms but is shy-flowering. It is grown for its beautiful woolly silver-grey foliage, which contrasts superbly with golden-foliage heathers. Very compact, low grower to a height of 25cm (10in). Plant five per m² (sq yd).

'Sir John Charrington'
Dark crimson blooms but grown primarily for its golden-orange foliage which, in winter, takes on red tints. It has quite a spreading habit and attains a height of 40cm (15in). Plant three per m² (sq yd).

'Sister Anne'
This is an ideal variety for ornamental containers: it has pink flowers in profusion and attractive grey woolly foliage. Very compact and low growing, no more than 10cm (4in) in height. Plant seven per m² (sq yd).

'Sunset'
Produces pink blooms, but rather sparsely. Grown primarily for its colourful foliage: yellow, gold and orange. Rather loose in habit and attaining a height of 30cm (12in). Plant five per m² (sq yd).

'Tib'
The double flowers are rose-red and make a fine display, set against their dark green foliage. A tall, vigorous, erect yet compact variety, up to 60cm (2ft) in height. Plant five per m² (sq yd).

'Wickwar Flame'
The flowers are lavender-coloured. Grown mainly for its foliage, which is orange-yellow in summer and brilliant orange-red in winter. A compact grower, no more than 30cm (12 in) in height. Plant five per m² (sq yd).

Calluna vulgaris 'Sister Anne'

Daboecia cantabrica 'Alba', a reliably vigorous flowerer

Daboecia cantabrica

(St Dabeoc's heath) This is a distinctive heath with a bushy habit of growth. It can grow up to 90cm (3ft) in height, although varieties are generally shorter. The bell-shaped flowers are larger than other heathers and so, too, are the leaves, which are elliptical in shape, pointed, hard, and dark green with silvery undersides. It must be grown in moist, acid soils. Generally, varieties are grown, rather than the species.

'Alba'

Produces a good display of white flowers. Foliage same as species; height 60cm (2ft). Plant five of this variety per m^2 (sq yd).

'Atropurpurea'

Produces a fine display of dark purple flowers. The foliage is flushed with bronze; height 60cm (2ft). Plant five per m^2 (sq yd).

'Praegerae'

Produces long, semi-pendulous spikes of dark pink flowers. The foliage is bright mid-green; height 30cm (12in). Plant five of these per m^2 (sq yd).

'William Buchanan'

Produces a fine display of crimson flowers and shiny foliage of a dark green. Vigorous habit but only 30cm (12in) in height. You will need to plant five per m^2 (sq yd).

Erica cinerea 'Hockstone White' is the largest white flowered form

Erica ciliaris
(Dorset heath) Varieties of the Dorset heath are popular for heather beds and mixed planting. They have a low carpeting habit of growth and make good ground cover. Bell-shaped flowers, freely produced over a long period. Grow in acid soil.

'Mrs C. H. Gill'
Produces a good display of red flowers set against dark green foliage. Carpeting habit, to a height of 30cm (12in). Plant four or five per m^2 (sq yd).

'Stoborough'
Long spikes of white flowers and vivid green foliage. Vigorous grower, attaining a height of 60cm (2ft). Plant four or five per m^2 (sq yd).

Erica cinerea
(Bell heather) The varieties are highly popular for heather beds and mixed plantings, forming low carpets or mats and making excellent ground cover. The bell-shaped flowers are generally very freely produced. Must have an acid soil.

'Atrosanguinea Smith's Variety'
A highly recommended variety which produces an impressive display of scarlet flowers. Dark green foliage. Spreading habit; height 15-20cm (6-8in). Plant five per m^2 (sq yd).

'C. D. Eason'
Definitely one of the very best varieties, with bold spikes of bright red-pink flowers against a background of deep green foliage. Bushy habit; 30cm (12in) high. Plant five per m^2 (sq yd).

'Cevennes'
Creates a spectacular display of lavender-rose blooms set against light green foliage. Has a rather erect habit, to a height of 22-30cm (9-12in). Plant five per m^2 (sq yd).

'Golden Drop'

Produces a sparse crop of pink flowers. Primarily a foliage variety, it is coppery-gold in summer and flushed with red in winter. Prostrate habit of growth; height 15cm (6in). Plant five per m^2 (sq yd).

'Hockstone White'

Produces long spikes of white flowers – considered to be the best white variety – with vivid green foliage. Vigorous, erect habit, to a height of 45cm (18in). Plant four per m^2 (sq yd).

'Pink Ice'

The flowers are bright pink and set against dark green foliage, which is flushed with bronze in the winter and spring. Bushy but very compact in habit, growing to a height of 25cm (10in). Plant five per m^2 (sq yd).

'Purple Beauty'

Makes a good display of bright purple flowers and has dark green foliage. A bushy vigorous plant; height 25cm (10in). Plant five per m^2 (sq yd).

'Velvet Night'

Well recommended for its unusual colour: very dark black-purple flowers against mid-green foliage. Spreading habit, attaining a height of 30cm (12in). Plant five per m^2 (sq yd).

'Windlebrooke'

The purple flowers are rather sparse but this is essentially a foliage variety: light gold in summer and changing to orange-red in winter. It has a spreading habit and attains a height of 25cm (10in). Plant five per m^2 (sq yd) for the best effect.

Erica cinerea 'Windlebrook' has spectacular foliage colour in winter

Erica terminalis (E. stricta, E. corsica)

(Corsican heath) A tall, stiff, erect shrub up to 2.4m (8ft) in height with a spread of 1.2m (4ft). The dark pink blooms turn russet-brown when they die and can be left for winter effect. The dense foliage emerges brilliant green and eventually becomes dark green. The stems are rather brittle and can be damaged by falls of snow. Sometimes grown as a hedge. This species thrives in alkaline soils.

Erica tetralix

(Cross-leaved heath) A distinctive heath whose greyish-green leaves cross over each other, hence the common name. Despite a rather loose, spreading habit of growth, it makes acceptable ground cover. A very attractive foliage plant which also flowers well, associating particularly well with golden-foliage heathers. Must be grown in acid soil. Grows in wet places in the wild and, in the garden, must have moisture-retentive soil. Generally, the numerous varieties are grown.

'Alba Mollis'

White flowers set against conspicuous silver-grey foliage. Spreading and rather loose habit, attaining a height of 30cm (12in). Plant five per m² (sq yd).

'Con Underwood'

Produces quite large crimson blooms set against grey-green foliage. Spreading and rather loose habit, attaining a height of 25cm (10in). Plant five per m² (sq yd).

'Pink Star'

Provides an excellent display of pink flowers set against smoky grey foliage. Spreading and rather loose habit, attaining a height of 20cm (8in). Plant five per m² (sq yd).

Erica tetralix 'Con Underwood'

Erica vagans

(Cornish heath) This is a vigorous, bushy heath found growing wild in Britain, and producing bold spikes of flowers over a long period. The dead flowers turn russet-brown and can be left for winter effect. Best grown in acid soils but will tolerate *slightly* alkaline conditions. Varieties are grown and are considered indispensible for the heather bed or mixed plantings.

'Cream'

Makes a marvellous display of cream-white flowers, set against dark green foliage. Very vigorous, bushy habit, attaining a height of 50cm (20in). Plant five per m² (sq yd).

'Lyonesse'

White flowers with contrasting brown anthers. Vivid green foliage. Very vigorous, attaining a height of 45cm (18in). For a good display, plant five per m² (sq yd).

Rose-pink blooms of the delightful *Erica vagans* 'St Keverne'

Erica vagans 'Valerie Proudley'

'Mrs D. F. Maxwell'
This is one of the top ten heathers and should be in every garden! Deep rose-pink blooms, with conspicuous dark brown anthers, and dark green foliage. Very vigorous, attaining a height of 45cm (18in). Plant five per m^2 (sq yd).

'St Keverne'
Makes a marvellous display of rose-pink blooms with contrasting dark brown anthers. The foliage is dark green. Bushy but compact habit, attaining a height of 50cm (20in). Plant five per m^2 (sq yd).

'Valerie Proudley'
A good variety for ornamental containers due to its small size, it has white flowers and golden foliage which is attractive throughout the year. This slow-growing variety, of compact habit, attains a height of 15-20cm (6-8in). Plant six of this variety per m^2 (sq yd).

41

AUTUMN

Calluna vulgaris

(Ling) A very well-known heather found growing wild in several parts of Britain. Distinguished by its very small, scale-like leaves, it has a low carpet- or mat-forming habit, making excellent ground cover. The flowers are carried in long spikes. Can only be grown in acid soils. The species itself is rarely grown, but there are hundreds of varieties and some of these are at their best in the autumn. Good as cut flowers.

'H. E. Beale'

This is one of the best-known heathers and very widely planted. The double flowers are very good for cutting and arranging indoors. They are silvery pink and held in bold sprays. The foliage is also attractive, being grey-green and, in winter, flushed with mauve. Young plants provide the best flower display so replace regularly. Height 60cm (2ft). Plant five per m^2 (sq yd).

'My Dream'

This variety makes a superb display with its double, white flowers, set against mid-green foliage. It has an upright, bushy habit and attains a height of 60cm (2ft). Plant five per m^2 (sq yd).

'Peter Sparkes'

Like 'H. E. Beale', this is one of the best-known heathers and should be in every garden. It makes a superb display of double, dark pink flowers. The foliage is mid-green. Attains 45cm (18in). Plant five per m^2 (sq yd).

Calluna vulgaris 'H. E. Beale', a good double-flowered variety

Erica × *darleyensis* 'Arthur Johnson'; vigorous and reliable

WINTER

Erica* × *darleyensis
(Winter-flowering heather) A hybrid, forming mats or carpets of foliage; excellent ground-cover and flowers over a very long period. Only varieties are grown; suitable for planting in alkaline soils.

'Arthur Johnson'
Produces long spikes of rose-pink flowers and has pleasant mid-green foliage. A strong-growing variety, attaining a height of 60-90cm (2-3ft) when in flower. Plant three per m^2 (sq yd).

'George Rendall'
Makes a good display with its deep pink flowers. The foliage is attractive, too, as the shoot tips are creamy-pink in the spring and in early summer. This quite wide-spreading variety attains a height of 45cm (18in). You will need to plant only three per m^2 (sq yd).

'Ghost Hills'
This variety blooms profusely, making a long and marvellous display with its dark pink flowers. In the spring the tips of the young shoots are cream in colour. Quite a wide-spreading variety, it attains a height of 40cm (15in). Plant three per m^2 (sq yd).

'Silberschmelze' ('Molten Silver')
This is undoubtedly the best white variety, being very popular and widely planted. Very long spikes of white flowers against a background of dark green foliage. This is a particularly vigorous, wide-spreading variety, attaining a height of 45cm (18in), so you need to plant just three per m^2 (sq yd).

Erica herbacea (E. carnea)

(Winter-flowering heather) Mat-forming plant making excellent ground cover and with a very long flowering period. Excellent for alkaline soils but if the soil is very thin, add a large amount of peat. Only varieties are grown but there are many to choose from.

'Eileen Porter'

This variety creates a carpet of bright red flowers over a very long period. The foliage is dark green and makes a good background for the blooms. It is a spreading, prostrate variety, attaining a height of 20cm (8in). Plant five per m^2 (sq yd).

'January Sun'

This is an ideal variety for ornamental containers. The pink flowers are rather sparse but this is primarily a foliage variety; the foliage is gold. A small and very compact grower, no more than 10cm (4in) in height. Plant six to eight per m^2 (sq yd).

Erica herbacea 'Pink Spangles'

Pink, tussock-forming *Erica herbacea* 'King George'

'King George'

Although an old variety this is still very popular and highly rated. It flowers profusely, bearing rose-pink blooms over a very long period and the dark green foliage makes a good background for the flowers. A compact plant, attaining a height of 20cm (8in). Plant five per m^2 (sq yd).

'Pink Spangles'

The extra-large flowers are deep pink and produced in abundance; dark green foliage. It is a strong-growing, wide-spreading variety, reaching a height of 20cm (8in). Plant three per m^2 (sq yd).

'Praecox Rubra'

Produces an abundance of small, dark rose-red flowers set against mid- to dark green foliage. It is a prostrate variety, to 15cm (6in) in height. Plant five per m^2 (sq yd).

'Springwood Pink'

One of the most popular and widely planted varieties, making superb ground cover and also recommended for planting in ornamental containers. The mass of pink flowers is produced against a background of dark green foliage. A strong grower, it attains a height of 20cm (8in). Plant three per m^2 (sq yd).

Erica herbacea 'Springwood Pink' makes a good container plant

Another erica for containers, *Erica herbacea* 'Springwood White'

'Springwood White'

This variety is as popular as 'Springwood Pink' and makes excellent ground cover. It is also recommended for growing in ornamental containers. It produces sheets of white flowers with conspicuous brown anthers and the foliage is vivid green, so it is a good companion plant suitable for a variety of colour schemes. A strong grower, forming wide mats and attaining a height of 20cm (8in). You will need only to plant three per m^2 (sq yd).

'Vivellii'

This also is one of the most popular of the *herbacea* varieties, producing an abundance of brilliant carmine flowers. The foliage is dark green but in winter is heavily flushed with bronze. Quite a strong-growing, spreading plant, it attains a height of 20cm (8in). Plant five of this variety per m^2 (sq yd).

GOOD FOLIAGE PLANTS

Coloured or attractive foliage is one of the major features of heaths and heathers. Many varieties which have notable foliage have been included in the descriptive lists. However, they are listed here for quick reference. Of course, all have been fully described in the lists.

SPRING

Erica arborea
E.a. 'Alpina'
Erica × *darleyensis* 'Jack H. Brummage'
Erica erigena 'Brightness'
E.e. 'W. T. Rackliff'
Erica herbacea 'Ann Sparkes'
E.h. 'Aurea'
E.h. 'Foxhollow'
E.h. 'Loughrigg'
E.h. 'Westwood Yellow'
Erica lusitanica
Erica umbellata
Erica × *veitchii* 'Exeter'

SUMMER

Calluna vulgaris 'Beoley Gold'
C.v. 'Blazeaway'
C.v. 'Boskoop'
C.v. 'Elsie Purnell'
C.v. 'Gold Haze'
C.v. 'Golden Carpet'
C.v. 'Joy Vanstone'
C.v. 'Multicolor'
C.v. 'Orange Queen'
C.v. 'Robert Chapman'
C.v. 'Silver Queen'
C.v. 'Sir John Charrington'
C.v. 'Sister Anne'
C.v. 'Sunset'
C.v. 'Wickwar Flame'
Daboecia cantabrica 'Atropurpurea'
Erica cinerea 'Golden Drop'
E.c. 'Pink Ice'
E.c. 'Windlebrooke'
Erica terminalis
Erica tetralix – all varieties
Erica vagans 'Valerie Proudley'

AUTUMN

Calluna vulgaris 'H. E. Beale'

WINTER

Erica × darleyensis 'George Rendall'
E. × d. 'Ghost Hills'
Erica herbacea 'January Sun'
E.h. 'Vivellii'

C.v. 'Sir John Charrington'

Calluna vulgaris 'Sunset' has beautiful foliage colour all year round

INDEX AND ACKNOWLEDGEMENTS

Picture credits

Pat Brindley: 33(t), 34.
John Glover: 1, 36(t).
Harry Smith Collection: 4/5, 7, 9(b), 15, 16, 20(t,b), 21(b), 22, 25, 32(b), 33(b), 41(b), 43.
Michael Warren: 6, 8, 14, 17, 18, 19, 21(t), 23(t,b), 24, 28/9, 30(t,b), 31, 32(t), 35, 36(b), 37, 38, 39, 40, 41(t), 42/3, 44(t,b), 45, 46, 47(t,b).

Artwork by Simon Roulstone